REDEEM
YOUR ROOTS

REDEEM
YOUR ROOTS

Bridging the gap between nostalgia
and the next generation.

7 Keys to **Connect** to Your
Heritage, **Create** a Richer Life,
and **Continue** Your Legacy

DAWN MATTERA CORSI

Published by A Worthy Press
aworthypress.com

Library of Congress Control Number: 2024921631
Paperback: 978-1-956673-84-5
Hardcover: 978-1-956673-16-6
E-book: 978-1-956673-17-3
Available in hardcover, paperback, and e-book.

To protect the privacy of those who have shared their stories with the author, some details and names have been changed. Any Internet addresses (websites, blogs, etc.) printed in this book are offered as a resource. They are not intended in any way to be or imply an endorsement by the publisher, nor does the publisher vouch for the content of these sites for the life of this book.

Get Your FREE Guide!

5 Ways to
Boost Your
Happiness
in
5 Minutes...
Italian Style!

dawnmattera.com/boost-happiness

This book is dedicated to:

First and foremost, my grandparents for their courage, perseverance, and sacrifices made so that we could be where we are today.

May we never forget.

Anyone who wants to connect to their heritage or who's already keeping the flame of tradition burning.

May we inspire the next generation.

And, of course, my husband, Bob, as well as my siblings, cousins, and other assorted family members—blood-related or not—who truly make my life a *dolce vita*.

May we continue to learn, live, and love together!

Contents

Preface

"You don't stumble upon your heritage. It's there, just waiting to be explored and shared."
— Robbie Robertson

Dinner at Grandma's wasn't just a meal. It was a marathon, especially during the holidays. The house looked like a bakery had exploded with cookies and pies everywhere. She made both the traditional Italian and American holiday foods. Yeah, both. So, you can understand why my brother and I skipped breakfast.

Each course was more delicious than the last, and Grandma served generous portions. "Have-a some more, have-a some more," she'd exclaim, "You too skinny. Have-a some more!"

Sometimes, we'd have a guest who joined us for the first time at Grandma's table. They would say something ridiculous like, "Oh, no thank you. I'm full."

If you're of Italian heritage, you just gasped because you know what happened next.

Grandma would push herself away from the table, one hand on her heart and the other hand to the heavens, and proclaim, "Take-a me now, *Gesù*', take-a me now! I'm a failure. They no like-a my cooking. Take-a me now!"

And so we would all have-a some more!

You probably have similar memories of days gone by, and I know they're bittersweet. While we feel the warmth of being in a close-knit (and maybe a bit crazy) community, we also feel the loss of something that will never happen again. Worse, we may believe that our heritage—the root of who we are—and the sacrifices our ancestors made will be forgotten.

The good news is that it's not too late. You and I can revive our traditions and share our histories so that the next generation will carry the torch.

Let's never forget what our parents and grandparents did so that you and I could be where we are today. They deserve the recognition and it's our duty and honor to keep the memories alive.

You and I can bridge the gap from nostalgia to the next generation.

Introduction

The Importance of Redeeming Your Roots

"A family is only as strong as their stories."
~ Adriana Trigiani, *The Good Left Undone*

Maybe, like me, you want to be sure that your heritage is not forgotten. Or, maybe your family didn't practice the Old World or Native traditions but you want to learn about them now. Perhaps you married into a culture different than yours, or a DNA test uncovered an ethnicity that you'd like to explore.

No matter your motivation, you can discover and celebrate your rich cultural heritage and be inspired to share it with others. Plus, it's fulfilling and fun!

Connecting to Your Heritage

With today's technology, it's relatively easy to learn about cultural customs, traditions, and histories. A quick internet search will yield a myriad of responses to your questions.

As you dive deeper, you'll gain an appreciation for your ancestors and how they overcame challenges. Knowing that their DNA is in you can provide a source of strength in difficult times. You'll better understand their values and increase your sense of identity.

Connecting to your roots is fundamentally about learning. So, channel your inner Inspector Montalbano (an Italian TV detective) and get ready for some *Ah-ha!* moments.

Creating a Life You Love

This is where the fun begins! It's your choice of which traditions to include in your day-to-day activities, and they will lead you to a *dolce vita* (sweet life).

Whether you're trying a new recipe or filling out the branches of your family tree, you will be adding depth and interest to your life. Redeeming your roots may even shape your perspective about your purpose and how you fit into the world, especially when you get involved with other people and groups that share your passions.

Because my husband and I *live* these 7 Keys, which I'll introduce to you in the following

chapters, our lives are richer. Through genealogical research and travel (two of the 7
Keys), we've "discovered" family and made new
friends in Italy. By participating in social groups,
we learn and laugh with like-minded people.
You too can have a more meaningful and fulfilling life by following just one or two of the Keys
presented in this book.

This heritage quest might even inspire you or
your loved ones to pursue certain goals, interests, or careers. Maybe your niece will embrace
her desire to cook or plant a garden, and your
cousins will finally plan that trip of a lifetime.
Or, like me, you'll go from a Defense Industry Engineer to a Professional Italian-American.
(No, it's not an official title, but I might just add
that to my business card.)

Continuing the Legacy

Do you have children, grandchildren, nieces or
nephews? Do you love them and want the best
for them? Of course, you do!

Research[1] shows that children who learn their
family histories have greater resilience, confi-
dence, and sense of security. They learn values
and life lessons that will guide them today and

tomorrow. Who wouldn't want that for the next generation?

Michael Graziano, a professor at Princeton University's Neuroscience Institute, says, "Successful families often have examples of resilience — stories of obstacles faced and conquered together — woven through the family narrative."[2]

Yes, our children and grandchildren will reap the benefits of learning about their ancestors. Furthermore, our parents and grandparents deserve the honor and recognition for the commitments and sacrifices they made so you and I could be where we are today.

I understand that some of our families' stories may be embarrassing and even shameful. Heck, my family tree is full of nuts! I'm certainly not suggesting that we portray all our ancestors as saints and heroes. If there are stories of redemption, by all means, share them. But, even if your ancestry includes some "bad apples", this is your opportunity to ensure that the negative narrative stops today. You write the next chapter of your family's legacy.

What if you don't have children to pass this all on to, or what if they don't seem to care?

At the very least, you can contribute to your community and make a difference there. And, those grandkids, nieces, nephews, and godchildren who only are mesmerized by electronics today might have their interest sparked in the future. Don't let them down!

Believe it or not, some young people *do* have a desire to explore their heritage now. For example, Italian American Future Leaders is a non-profit organization of young adults whose goals are to "promote our shared traditions, uphold our heritage," and bridge the gap between older and younger Italian Americans.[3] That's just one of many such networks.

So, you see, there is hope.

Each of the following chapters will highlight one of the 7 Keys to Redeem Your Roots. They range from the easiest to accomplish and proceed to the most involved.

For each Key, we'll discuss the three C's, which are how to:

CONNECT to your heritage so you can

CREATE a life you love, and then

CONTINUE the legacy for the future.

You'll also read about people who not only embraced a Key but also took it to what I call "Over the Top!" The tales of these brave souls who went above and beyond will inspire you to take your next steps.

As a second-generation Italian-American, you won't be surprised that my stories and suggestions are tied to my heritage. But it doesn't matter where your ancestors came from because you can employ the same principles. I've even met with someone whose "heritage" they're connecting to, creating, and continuing is their religion.

So, whether you're of Mexican, Mandarin, or even Mandalorian descent, this book will help you bridge the gap from nostalgia to the next generation.

Andiamo! (Let's go!)

Chapter 1

Mangia! (Eat!): Your Heritage through Food

"Life is a combination of magic and pasta."
~ Federico Fellini

Think back to your grandma's kitchen. Mmm mm...remember the aroma of cookies baking or sauce simmering. The air was filled with intoxicating scents—and with love.

The easiest and most delicious way to connect, create, and continue your heritage is through food.

Mangiamo! (Let's eat!)

CONNECT

Maybe you enjoy family recipes that have been passed down from generation to generation. Or, perhaps you're the chef reviving interest in your culture, so you're exploring new-to-you dishes. Either way, indulging in ethnic specialties is a fun and appetizing way to start redeeming your roots.

It's fairly easy to find recipes and restaurants that offer authentic fare. For the latter, I'd suggest avoiding chains and trying smaller, mom-and-pop-type establishments. Not only will the food be better, but would also be supporting local businesses. Having lunch at the "Garden of Olives" won't mean much to their CEO, but stopping by the neighborhood bakery or pizzeria might help keep the owner's child in piano lessons.

As a side note, neighbors helping neighbors is an important part of the Italian culture; it's called *campanilismo*. It stems from the Italian word for "bell tower", *campanile*. It implies that anyone whose home shares a view of the same bell tower is your *paesano*, your compatriot. You probably share the same values and can trust one another. You'll stick together and help each other out.

You can find restaurants and recipe ideas through social groups, both in-person and online. Joining these organizations will expand your horizons in so many ways beyond just the culinary aspect. Be careful, though, because it might also expand your waistline!

In many cultures, breaking bread together is an important way to connect with others. It's not just about the food; it's about what happens *around* the food. At the table, share our day-to-day lives, our stories of the past, and our hopes for the future. It's where we can talk about Grandpa as we pour wine from his decanter. Or, we can tell an inspiring story about an aunt or cousin when we make her famous meatballs.

CREATE

The easiest thing to make for dinner is a reservation!

When you go to a restaurant, step out of your comfort zone by trying something you've never had before, or maybe sit at the bar where you might—gasp!—talk to other people. Remember that, at least in the Italian culture, starting up conversations with a stranger sitting beside you is normal and could lead to lifelong friendships. And, according to Blue Zone[4] experts, strong social interactions lead to a longer, healthier life.

There's something special, though, about cooking and baking at home, especially if it's a recipe that was handed down from past generations. You might need to shop at a specialty grocery store for some of the ingredients, but that's part of the adventure. There are so many celebrity chefs that you can follow for step-by-step instructions.

Some of my favorite online Italian cooks (who speak English) include Pasquale Sciarappa, Vincenzo Prosperi of Vincenzo's Plate, Nick Stellino, and the Pasta Grannies.[5] That last one isn't exactly a cooking channel but rather a show in which the host chronicles pasta-making grandmas from all over Italy. Trust me, you'll love it!

Think outside the (pasta) box and bring a chef into your kitchen. Yes, it's a thing. Just do an online search for "Italian chefs cook in your home" and you'll find someone in your area. For example, there's the Cucinamore chef in Virginia who will travel in a 35-mile radius[6], and the Traveling Italian Chef covers New Jersey up through Massachusetts[7]. I'd be remiss if I left out my friend from Abruzzo, Chef Ezio, who will not only create culinary magic in your (Rhode Island) kitchen but also offers—in his words—"secret and fabulous" tours in Italy.[8]

Another way to create a richer life through food—well, through drink—is the Neapolitan custom called *caffè sospeso*. The literal translation is "suspended coffee" which creates pictures of floating coffee cups in our imaginations. In reality, it's the Neapolitan version of paying it forward. To participate, you simply order two coffees and take only one. The second cup is "suspended" for another person, usually someone in need, financially or emotionally.

So, the next time you're in the drive-thru, pay for the car behind you. Or, at a restaurant, pick up the tab for that solo diner at the counter. Remember, though, that the only way that karma will smile upon you is when you do it anonymously. Well, unless the person in the car behind you is kinda cute, it wouldn't be a bad idea to make your act of charity known. But, I digress.

CONTINUE

Who doesn't like food? If they don't, then they're weird, right? Your kids, grandkids, nieces, and nephews might not want to try tripe, made from cow's stomach (me, neither!), but it's almost guaranteed that they'll like pizza.

The obvious option is to go out to a pizzeria or bring some pies home for a movie or game night. But a more interesting and much more fun idea is to make pizza at home. You can find numerous pre-recorded tutorials online, but I prefer live instruction. I'm sure there are classes near you that are fun for the whole family. But what if you're like me and the younger generation lives in a galaxy far, far away? Then, use the Force or, rather, video conferencing.

That's what I did with my great-nieces who live 12+ hours away from me. I enrolled us all in a pasta-making class with an honest-to-goodness grandmother (*nonna*) in Italy.[9] Before the class, I sent the girls some cooking tools and red aprons with their names embroidered on them; mine says "Aunt Dawn". Having *Nonna* right there on the screen with us was fantastic! She made custom suggestions so our ravioli came out perfect. It felt authentic, too. Later, my nephew texted that their youngest continued making more pasta. Maybe she caught the cooking bug!

Keep in mind, that connecting with the next generation doesn't have to be a big production. In fact, it's probably best when it happens naturally as a part of everyday life.

My brother Keith remembers when he'd stay over at Grandma's house and arrive late after work or being out with his buddies. (She lived alone and needed help getting in and out of bed, etc.) She'd wait up for him and offer to make him a snack. At first, he'd refuse, thinking he was being polite. If you read the Introduction, then you know what Grandma's response was: "You no like-a my cooking!" So, of course, Keith learned to agree to take her up on the offer.

Grandma was in a wheelchair for the last decade of her life, but it never stopped her from doing what she loved. Keith describes how she'd zoom over to the fridge, pile ingredients on her lap, and then wheel over to the stove. The aroma of garlic and love filled the kitchen.

Keith was a young man at the time, and instead of shooting hoops with the guys or flirting with the girls, he was in his grandmother's kitchen—and loving it. Especially now that we're in our sixties, he treasures those late nights listening to Grandma's stories.

You too can connect with your loved ones over a plate of pasta or a cup of coffee. Who knows? You might be making memories that the younger generation will talk about decades from now. Don't dismiss the magic that can happen in the simplest situations.

Just for fun, here are some rules and interesting facts about Italian Cuisine:

- Never put pineapple on pizza.

- Don't have a cappuccino after 11:00 am

- Caesar salad doesn't exist in Italy.

- Don't put cheese on seafood.

- Never put pineapple on pizza.

- If you order a "latte" in Italy, you'll get a glass of milk.

- There's no "x" in *espresso*.

- Chicken and veal parmigiana don't exist in Italy, only eggplant.

- *Never* put pineapple on pizza.

**Key #1: Food
Over the Top!**

Bella Napoli, Kansas City, Missouri

Let's meet Jake Imperiale in the Brookside area of Kansas City, Missouri. Many years ago, Jake opened a coffee shop, deli, and Italian import market called *Bella Napoli*. I especially loved visiting the store when his sister Vanda was cooking peppers. *Che bel profumo!* (What an aroma!)

When the space next door became available, Jake wanted to expand the family business. He took the time to travel to his mother's birthplace of Naples, Italy, to learn from the experts about how to make pizza.

These days, *Bella Napoli* is still a coffee shop, deli, and market, but also a warm and welcoming restaurant with the best pizzas and handmade pasta in the Midwest.[10]

Chapter 2

Eat, Pray, Love, and Eat Some More: Your Heritage through Holidays and Traditions

"Tradition is not the worship of ashes but the
preservation of fire."
~ Gustav Mahler

A man was watching his wife prepare a ham for dinner. She cut off a little from one end, a little from the other end, and then placed what was left in the baking pan. Curious, he asked about her technique.

His wife replied, "This is how my mother taught me, so that's how I do it. You'll have to ask her why."

Wanting to know the secret behind the mysterious ham hacking, he called his mother-in-law. She had a familiar response. "That's how my mother always did it. You'll have to ask her."

The man then called his wife's grandmother and recounted the conversations with his wife and mother-in-law. "Why," he implored, "do you cut both ends off the ham before baking it?"

Grandma laughed and offered her profound explanation: "My pan is too small!"

More than likely, your traditions are a bit more meaningful than the Ham Family's. No matter what or why, learning about our ethnic customs is another Key to Redeem Your Roots.

And, it's not just for the holidays. I'll share some of the traditions from Italy—everything from gardens to gifts for your "second" birthday—that might be a springboard for you to discover more about your cultural traditions.

CONNECT

A quick online search for "(insert ethnicity) traditions" will produce an infinite number of responses. You can narrow down the query by adding keywords like "birthday" or "summer". Pick the ones that catch your attention.

Aside from holidays, there are other ways to celebrate traditions. Think about your grandparents favorite pastimes. For example, mine had a huge garden, Grandma sewed and crocheted, and Grandpa made wine. We can learn to crochet and make wine today. I could plant a garden—if only I had a green thumb! Yeah, I'm more like a hospice for plants. I'll talk to them and love them, but they're going to the Great Nursery in the Sky.

I realize that some of you might not have those memories to recall; you're starting this heritage quest from scratch. Again, online searches and getting involved with cultural groups (see Chapter 7) will provide you with helpful information. Keep in mind that you'll discover a *lot* of choices. Don't get analysis paralysis; just pick one or two and go!

Here are two unique traditions from the land of my forefathers:

- *Onomastico*: This is known as your Name Day, and it's like a bonus birthday with heartfelt wishes and maybe even presents. The good news is that you don't have to add another candle to the cake! For example, June 24th is St John's Day. So anyone named John, Joan, or another variation is celebrated on that day.

- *La Befana*: A legend tells of the Three Wise Men who stopped at a woman's humble home for food and shelter. They invited her to join them as they followed the star to the newborn Messiah, but she declined because she was too busy. After they left, she realized the missed opportunity and set out to find them, but she never did. That woman became known as *La Befana*, a kindly witch who still seeks the Messiah and brings gifts to good boys and girls on the eve of Epiphany.

Some traditions have nothing to do with a date on the calendar, but instead with the art of living or a philosophy of life. For example, the Italian concept of *la bella figura* is more than its literal translation of "a good figure". It's important to look one's best because you are—like it or not—a representative of your family and community.

La bella figura is ingrained into the Italian psyche practically from birth. It's a mindset of making a good impression which is an extension of the Golden Rule. When we put our best foot forward, it certainly helps us, but it also extends respect and kindness to others.

Similarly, some treasured traditions are more accurately described as values. Below are a few of the most important ones in Italian culture and many others.

- Family

Family is not just about who you live with, but extends to a broader network which includes cousins, aunts, uncles, and even close family friends. Spending time together is important because generations share stories, celebrate traditions, and pass on values.

- Friendship

> *He who finds a friend finds a treasure.*
> ~ Italian Proverb

Friendships in Italian culture are profound connections that extend far beyond casual associations. They're woven into the very fabric of life, providing support, comfort, encouragement, and the occasional wake-up call. Friends are the family you choose.

- Faith

Many festivities are tied to religious events such as Easter and saints' days. (Ask anyone of Italian heritage if they've ever prayed to Saint Anthony when they lost something!)

Furthermore, churches aren't just places of worship; they also become social hubs. Everything from women's and men's groups to summer festivals and crafts all take place at the church and are offered to the parishioners and the whole community alike.

- Respect

Tying back to *la bella figura*, respect is shown to everyone...even if they're jerks! That's because your behavior is a reflection of you; what another person does is their business. I remember my father advising us, "Don't stoop to their level."

Respect is given especially to our elders who are highly esteemed for their wisdom and experience. Their advice is often sought and valued when making decisions.

- Work Ethic

Commitment to work, dedication, and striving for excellence are how we support our families and contribute to society. And, "work" includes at-home pursuits such as taking care of the house and growing vegetables. At the same time, balancing careers with personal life is important. While there may be times when the work-to-leisure ratio is skewed, we strive to spend our time so that we don't sacrifice one for the other.

- *Arrangiarsi*

One day, my uncle made a sad discovery: the barrels of Grandpa's wine in the cellar had turned to vinegar. Not only was it the last of what Grandpa had made, but it was disappointing to not be able to enjoy it. Uncle Johnny could've just poured it down the drain but he had an idea.

He sanitized dozens of Grandpa's small ceramic-topped wine bottles and filled them with the soured wine. He then set up a folding table on the sidewalk and taped to it a hand-written sign that read, "Organic Wine Vinegar." He sold every single bottle from his lemonade, um, vinegar stand!

That's an example of the spirit of *arrangiarsi*, a word that can't be fully translated into English. The literal meaning is "to arrange oneself", but it goes beyond that. It's the art of not only making the best of a situation but doing it in a clever way.

Another example of this is a cafè owner in Naples, Italy, who needed outdoor dining. He cut some circles out of wood and added box-like caps to the bottoms. He then placed the wooden discs on top of the posts that were meant to keep cars off the sidewalk. Ta-da! Instant outdoor tables.

Yes, life will throw us the occasional curveball. Let's figure out ways to find the silver lining, make the best of it, and turn it to our advantage if possible. At the very least, we acknowledge the plot twist and move on with our lives.

When life gives you lemons, make *limoncello*!

CREATE

You know what to do with this Key: incorporate your newfound traditions into the holidays and special events that you already celebrate. This might mean whipping up a recipe for *pastiera* at Easter or attending a midnight Mass on Christmas Eve.

Start to celebrate your loved ones' "second birthday", their *onomastico*. To find out when that occurs, simply do an online search for "Saint (Name) Day". You might have to take some artistic liberties if you can't find the exact name. For instance, there isn't a Saint Heather's Day. However, there is a National Heather Day in the United States on December 3rd. (Hey, I don't make these up; I'm just the messenger.)

You might also have to translate the name. For example, there isn't a Saint Dawn's Day, but there is a day for Our Lady of Alba. In Italian, *alba* means the beginning of the day, or dawn. In case you want to send me some dark chocolate on my *onomastico*, Saint Alba's Day is December 14th. I'm just kidding! (Or am I?)

Weaving these traditions into your life will be fun, heart-warming, and memorable.

CONTINUE

For those of you who are thinking, "Oh, my kids and grandkids don't care about our heritage," this part is just for you!

Who wouldn't want a second birthday? Even your adult children will gladly accept warm wishes (and even presents) as long as they don't have to put another candle on the cake. We continue this Key by celebrating your loved one's *onomastico*.

Speaking of birthdays, August 1st is my father's. Every year, my brother Keith and his son Max go to one of our dad's favorite places in Southern California. Not only is it a way of honoring Joe Mattera, but it also gives my brother the opportunity to talk about our dad and keep his memory alive in a low-key, natural way. Your ancestors' birthdays can be the perfect segue to remember your traditions and make them relevant today.

Another way to get the next generation interested in carrying on traditions is to include them in your holiday preparations. Ask them to physically help you or, at the very least, ask if they'd prefer "A" or "B". You never know what seed you may be planting, and you might be surprised when they're curious and ask to know more.

As you enjoy discovering your family's traditions, your enthusiasm will start to shine. Not only will your life become more enjoyable, but you'll inspire others to do the same.

Key #2: Holidays and Traditions Over the Top!

Italian Mass Project of New York

In 2021, Alexis N. Carra-Tracey founded a group dedicated to not only her Catholic faith but also to bringing together the Italian-American community through cultural renewal. The Italian Mass Project of New York[11] is run 100% by volunteer and hosts events from Masses in Italian to holiday celebrations like the Feast of the Seven Fishes.

One of their most popular events is their Tomato Sauce Day. Held at the end of August, participants gather to crush tomatoes and preserve hundreds of bottles of sauce. They start early in the morning, enjoy lunch together, and conclude with an English/Italian Mass.

Chapter 3

You Had Me at "Ciao!" Your Heritage through Language

If you can't say something nice, say it in Italian and smile!

My grandfather immigrated to America in the early 1920s, when his sweetheart was still far away in Italy. To keep the flames of love burning, he sent her postcards with romantic sentiments like "*Sei la mia stella*" ("You are my star"). It's okay to swoon here.

On a few of those postcards (which we found years after he passed away), he signed off with "*Gubai*". Huh? Even people who spoke my grandparents' dialect had no idea what *gubai* meant—until we said it out loud and used the Italian pronunciation. Phonetically, Grandpa had been saying "goo-BUY". In other words, "Goodbye."

Grandpa did his best to use his new American language, and I know it wasn't always easy. As a way to honor him, I can learn his first language. Plus, it adds another dimension to understanding and embracing my culture.

Learning a new language is not just about memorizing words and grammar rules. It's about immersing yourself in a culture, understanding its nuances, and appreciating its history. The echoes of our ancestors are in every syllable and it creates a sense of belonging to something bigger than ourselves.

Language is more than a means of communication. It's a link to our past, a tool for our present, and a gift for our future.

CONNECT

Before we dive into various methods of language learning, I'd like to address the subject of dialects. For example, my grandparents, father, and uncle spoke a Neapolitan dialect that was quite different from the Italian language. I never learned the dialect, which some may say is unfortunate. In reality, it turned out to be for the best because I still would've needed to learn Italian. A dialect isn't just an accent, like a southern drawl; it's often a distinctly separate language. For instance, there's even a Sicilian-Italian dictionary!

You might remember hearing words or phrases that are specific to a dialect and exclusive to the region your family came from. That doesn't mean those words are wrong, they're just not the textbook vocabulary, and that's okay. In fact, I think dialects are significant because they foster the bonds of a tight-knit group. Having said that, I don't understand 99 percent of what my family on the island of Ischia says when they speak the dialect.

A quick online search for "how to learn (language)" will produce numerous available resources. Which one is best for you? It depends on your learning style and your motivation.

If you're an auditory learner, just listening to an app or other recording will work for you. Many programs offer a free trial. However, if you learn best by seeing or doing something, you might look into video-based programs or in-person lessons. These days, you can even find native speakers who will teach you using video conferencing. Neither one of you has to leave the house! If your instructor lives in a different country, just remember the time difference; 5:00 p.m. for you might be midnight for them. So be open to meeting on your lunch breaks or Saturday mornings.

You'll also find excellent information on YouTube. Two of my favorite Italian language vloggers include *LearnAmo* and *Italiano Automatico*[12]. Although a bit advanced, I also enjoy *EfficaceMente* for the positive and practical messages about living life to the fullest[13]. That one doesn't include language lessons at all, but it's a great way to listen to a native speaker on a topic I enjoy.

Don't be too proud to use resources meant for children. Books, shows, websites, and other resources made for kids, many of which are bilingual, are also beneficial for us adults. No blankies or teddy bears required—unless you want one!

What if you want to pick up some Italian phrases for just a vacation or two? Look for lessons that are specifically for travelers or advertised as "conversational." If you're taking classes with a real-time instructor, let them know your goals.

As for your motivation, always know *why* you want to do something. And this is true for all your activities, whether it's conjugating verbs, losing weight, or building a business. There will be times when you're frustrated and tempted to quit. Remembering why you want to succeed will get you back on track.

Your motivation for learning a new language may evolve as you proceed on your heritage quest. For instance, my husband's Italian family lives in a small, hillside town with a population of less than 300. Very few of them speak English. My fluency has helped us establish a deeper connection with them, which in turn, makes our lives richer and more meaningful.

In the next chapter, connecting to your heritage through language is amped up with movies and music. But, in the spirit of this chapter, I suggest watching a movie that you already know and love and setting the language or subtitles to the one you're learning. Likewise, you can pick up a copy of a favorite book in your "new" foreign language. You get *cannoli* points (versus brownie points) for doing either of those!

CREATE

No matter what learning method you use, my biggest tip is to practice every day. It doesn't require a huge time commitment. Maybe listen to some music or read an online article. When you're at a stop light, say the characters of the license plate in front of you out loud, or try to recite your to-do list in your second language.

When I was first learning Italian (at almost age forty), I had little sticky notes all over the house. So when I went to the *frigo* (fridge) to get the *latte* (milk), the notes offered continuous reinforcement. Unfortunately, the label on my *cane* (dog) kept falling off.

Remember to keep this fun. If you start getting stressed about verbs or vocabulary, you won't continue, and consistency is key. It's like going to the gym: one time is not going to give me six-pack abs. Learning a language requires regularly exercising that mental muscle: your brain. We're more likely to press on if we're having a good time doing it.

One of my favorite ways to practice *la bella lingua* (the beautiful language) is with conversation groups. When I lived in New Hampshire, the Bedford Italian Cultural Society met twice a week for conversation at the library[14]. When I moved two hours away, it wasn't practical to attend. However, a silver lining from 2020 was that the conversation group started meeting online. I now participate once a week with my *amici* (friends).

In Chapter 7, we'll look at additional benefits, aside from language, of being an active member of a cultural group.

CONTINUE

Oh, how I wish I'd learned Italian when I was young! Since we can't go back in time, we can help the next generation today.

As with every topic in this book, it's best to try not to shove our newfound ethnic enthusiasm down the throats of our kids and grandkids. Think how you'd feel if they were in your face about their favorite pop star or influencer. Blech! Also, before I get any nastygrams, you might want to check with their parents first, if they're not your children.

The younger the child, the easier it will be. You can share music and books that are specifically made for their age range. A company that comes highly recommended is the Italian Children's Market whose tagline is "Give the gift of heritage." They have everything from toys to jewelry, as well as products for grown-ups.

As we share stories of our ancestors, we can include the occasional word or phrase even if it is in the dialect. For example, I can wipe the counter with a *moppine* (dish towel) and talk about my grandmother who always said that word. Remember that the goal of this book is to keep our heritage and ancestors' memories alive. Language—spoken and written—has long been a key to achieving that goal.

Key #3: Language Over the Top!

Scuola Leonardo da Vinci (Italian Language School)

Many adults think they're too old to learn a new language. While it is easier for children, you *can* teach an old dog new tricks. It may be *ruff*, but it will be worth it.

Even though I took Italian in high school, I was more interested in having fun than studying. My apologies to Ms. Rizzo at Classical High School! I was almost forty when I started taking it seriously, attending group language lessons before my first trip to Italy.

After meeting my family across the Atlantic, I realized that only one person there spoke English, and only one person in the States spoke Italian. Once those family members passed away, our connection would eventually be lost. I didn't want to be one of the thousands who say, "We have family in Europe, but we don't know who they are." Someone needed to learn the language, so I nominated myself.

While continuing with group lessons in 2002 and beyond, I also studied at home with tapes and CDs. (Yes, I'm *that* old!) In 2004, I lived in Florence, Italy, for two months to attend a language school[15]. I lived with a widow who spoke no English and, when I was out and about, I let the locals know that I preferred to speak their language. Thanks to this immersion, my language skills increased from beginner to intermediate/advanced. I even passed the exam to earn a diploma in the language.

Learning Italian has opened doors that I could've never imagined including forming friendships all over the world, working with cultural organizations that align with my passions, and sharing my message of living a *dolce vita*.

If I did it, you can too!

Chapter 4

Serenades and Silver Screens: Your Heritage through Music and Film

"If music be the food of love, play on."
~ William Shakespeare, *Twelfth Night*

Music and film are universal languages that transcend borders and time. They're mirrors that reflect our past, present, and future, and can become keys to understanding our roots. They aren't just notes in the air or frames on a screen; they're bridges that can span generations, weaving the tapestry of our heritage with promises of the future.

There's probably a song that takes you back to a place and time so vivid that you can hear, smell and even taste the moment. Maybe it's the song that was played during your first dance with your partner, or the one blasted across the stadium when your team won the championship. After the first few notes, you remember your sweetheart's cologne or a sea of 30,000 flags waving in victory.

Whenever I hear "Walking on Sunshine" by Katrina and the Waves, my mind is instantly transported to Florence, Italy, as I made my way to the Scuola Leonardo da Vinci in 2004. Every morning, as I walked to class, I passed by an internet café. As they prepared to open for the day, that song was always on their playlist. Katrina will never know that her lyrics stir up feelings of adventure, courage, and joy in me.

What's your favorite movie, the one you could watch again and again? Mine is *It's a Wonderful Life*, and my second favorite is *La Vita è Bella (Life Is Beautiful)*. We love the stories they tell, in which a relatable character overcome tremendous odds. They inspire the hero who lives inside of us. And, yes, we all love some silly movies that just make us laugh. Drama or comedy, film is a powerful medium to share a message.

Music and film can help us understand our roots in an entertaining and, therefore, memorable way. This also makes our heritage quest easier and more interesting for the next generation.

As we explore the arts as a bridge to our past, remember that some facts may be exaggerated or even falsified while others are purposely omitted. Don't write a merciless message to the artist or director. Just glean what you want from the piece and move on. If something really gets your *mutande* ("undies") in a bunch, use it as an opportunity to teach others about it.

CONNECT

Thanks to technology, finding movies and music from your culture is relatively easy. If you can't find something online, you might be able to find it in your local library. Even if you live in a small town, your library is probably connected to a larger one. That's helpful because state- or county-run libraries often have a system that allows items to be requested from bigger branches and sent to your local library. No need to make a long trek to get that CD anymore. (Hey, at least I didn't say "8-track!")

Social groups and colleges often host film festivals and concerts. For example, the Italian Film Festival USA hosts an annual event with premieres shown in cities from Boston to Boulder and Pittsburgh to Phoenix[16]. Schools with a strong Italian language program, like Florida Atlantic University, sponsor films and public discussions directly tied to heritage[17]. Likewise, you can do a little research for events in your area. In Chapter 7, you'll find more resources.

In addition to *La Vita è Bella*, some Italian films and television series to get you started include *Cinema Paradiso*, *The Best of Youth*, and *My Brilliant Friend*. Of course, there are the works of Federico Fellini and anything starring Sophia Loren. Don't worry about the language. Many of them are already subtitled or your smart TV can translate for you. Dubbed versions are also sometimes available.

CREATE

It's easy to make music the backdrop to your day-to-day activities. Either download some tunes or find an online foreign radio[18] station. I realize that you might have to bribe your family to watch subtitled movies with you. It's okay if they make some lame excuse about why they can't; this can be your "alone" time. Also, English-speaking movies that take place in Italy (or wherever your family comes from) are abundant.

Sure, we could just hit the play button and watch or listen. But we can make it more interesting and memorable by stepping up our game.

- Find out what songs were popular the week your parents were born or the year your grandparents celebrated an anniversary. This could also give you insights into what was happening in the world at that time and expand your appreciation for your forebears.

- While you're cooking or having dinner (Chapter 1), have an ethnic song list to play in the background.

- Prepare foods that go along with the movie you're watching. For example, *La Vita e' Bella* takes place in Arezzo. So, you could enjoy some *peposo* (stew) or *porchetta* (roast pork) with a glass of Chianti.

CONTINUE

Obviously, the simplest way to involve the next generation is to invite them to watch or listen along with you. Yeah, I can picture their eyeballs rolling, too. So, how about if you listen to new (i.e. contemporary) music from the Old Country? Now I can picture *your* eyeballs rolling!

If we want our kids and grandkids to listen to our choices, shouldn't we be open to theirs? The next time they come over, maybe you could just happen to have Eurovision winners Maneskin playing. Or, plan a movie night that doesn't have to feature an oldie. As of this writing, there were numerous films released in the last year or so that took place in Italy including one from the *Mission Impossible* series.

You might remember reading in the Introduction that the chapters in this book are loosely ordered from easiest to most involved. But listening to music and watching some flicks doesn't take too much effort. So, why does this chapter come after ones about traditions and language? Because the next suggestion will take a lot more time and, if you hire someone to do it for you, a monetary investment.

One way to ensure that your family's history is preserved for many generations to come is with a video. (You could also write a memoir or biography. We'll look at that in Chapter 5 which is about genealogy.) There are companies that will make such a video for you. To find them, do an internet search for "family history video production."

Making a video yourself will take time and some tech savvy. Most home computers have video-making software already included, and you can find a lot of "b-roll" videos online to add interest and flair to your production. If you don't have photos of your ancestors, you can include images of their homeland, landmarks, and other stock photos.

From there, you can upload the video to YouTube where it will "live" forever, or close to it. Send the link to your kids, grandkids, and anyone else who will watch. For a gift to unwrap, download the video to a thumb drive rather than burning it to a disc. Not everyone has a DVD player these days, but we all have USB ports.

Not to get all elfin on you, but Galadriel (*The Lord of the Rings: The Fellowship of the Rings*) must've read my mind about our journey to re-deeming our roots: "This task was appointed to you," she says. "And if you do not find a way, no one will."

Okay, that is a bit dramatic. But really, what if you *are* the only one interested in preserving your family history? If not you, then who? If not now, when?

We can do this, my friend, and will be worth it!

Key #4: Music and Film
Over the Top!

The Soul of Sicily: Margie Raimondo

Margie Raimondo is a multi-talented individual as a chef, author, farmer, and filmmaker with roots in Sicily and Campania. Following a year spent in Italy, she was inspired to share the stories of Sicilian farmers and their enduring commitment to working the land despite numerous challenges. Her documentary, *The Soul of Sicily*, won several best short film awards, and Margie was honored as best producer at an indie film festival.

Margie, along with her partner Chris, operates Urbana Farmstead, a farmers' market, kitchen, and farm in Little Rock, Arkansas[19]. She keeps farming and food preservation traditions alive through cooking and canning classes as well as farm workshops. Her first cookbook, *Mangiamo*, was published in November 2022, and her latest book, *Finding Your Path*, was released in August 2024.

Chapter 5

Branching Out: Your Heritage through Genealogy

"We inherit from our ancestors gifts so often taken for granted. We are links between the ages, containing past and present expectations, sacred memories and future promise."
~ Edward Sellner

When you shake your family tree, do a bunch of nuts fall off? Maybe your ancestors' coat of arms ties at the back? No matter what you might find, there's been a revived interest in genealogy these last few years.

You've probably seen TV programs in which celebrities explore their family histories. And, we've all heard stories about DNA testing kits that have led to some beautiful discoveries...and some shocking surprises. Even dogs can have their heritage traced.

Genealogy isn't merely the study of family history and lineage, and it's more than just names and dates. It's a journey of discovery, where you'll learn stories of love, resilience, triumph, and even tragedy. These tales aren't just about your ancestors; they're about you. They're the threads that weave the fabric of your identity.

CONNECT

The best place to start is right at home. If you're blessed to have your parents or grandparents still around or older uncles and aunts, I encourage you—no, I *implore* you to ask them questions.

I would further suggest that you record their answers rather than rely on your memory. Ask them about when they were growing up, such as what a typical day was like or what was served at Sunday dinners. You might even bring some old photos to spark their memories of your relatives or holiday traditions.

Maybe you have their diaries or military paperwork. Be sure to dust off old Bibles because you might find important dates (like births, weddings, and deaths) written on the blank pages. You may also discover notes, prayer cards, and postcards. These are all clues to what and who they held dear.

Thanks to the internet, filling in the branches of your family tree is so much easier today than in the past. The online resources are almost infinite, and that includes official records both here and in Europe. Although there's nothing like holding Grandpa's birth certificate while in his hometown's records office, you can save a lot of time and money by accessing it electronically.

Many European immigrants came through Ellis Island. On their website, you can find ship manifests with interesting details such as your ancestors' occupations, their traveling companions, and where they stayed upon arrival[20]. Seeing a photo of the sailing vessel they took to come to America can spark your imagination about their adventure.

Keep in mind that an English-speaking clerk was transcribing your relative's broken English. So, names, places, and other information were sometimes close approximations. My grandfather's name was Ignazio. Yeah, you can assume they had to guess the correct spelling on that one.

On the ship manifests, take note of the names above and below your ancestors'. You might find a pleasant surprise like we did.

In May 1912, a ship named *Canada* arrived at Ellis Island. On board was my husband's great-grandfather, Francesco. According to the records, there was another young man from the same town in Italy: Dante Simone. However, when we first encountered this in our research, the trail went cold for Grandfather Francesco's traveling companion.

Fast-forward many decades to when my husband's family in Rhode Island is friends with Sal, who happens to have ancestors from the same small town in Italy. Throughout the years, they jokingly called him "cousin" because of that connection.

Well, it's no joke. Remember Dante Simone from the ship manifest? That was Sal's grandfather! I know: that doesn't make us related. However, when my husband and I traveled to that small town, we discovered that Sal is indeed family. The relationship is through marriage, but we're cousins just the same.

Not all immigrants came through Ellis Island; secondary ports in New York were Castle Island and the Barge Office. Other important landing points were Boston, Philadelphia, and Baltimore, which explains the large number of Italian Americans in those areas.

Many Italian immigrants also came in through New Orleans and then journeyed north on the Mississippi River. That's why when I lived in the Kansas City area, I was quite surprised to find so many Italians had settled in that part of the country.

I won't share the story here about Italians in New Orleans and the connection to Columbus Day. That's because I don't want to turn the focus of this book into a highly-charged debate. If you're of Italian heritage, I strongly encourage you to investigate the history. You can be proud of how our ancestors overcame adversity and persevered to become victors rather than victims.

Okay, I'm off my soap box. And, now, we return to our regularly scheduled program, um, book.

Most town halls (*comuni*) in Italy have websites, but not all have the option to order records. If they do, you'll need your ancestor's full name and date of birth (not just the year). Be aware that they are inundated with requests, and they have a responsibility to their residents who take first priority. You as a foreigner, will take a far distant second or third place when it comes to your records request. If you go to Italy, it can be a bit easier. More about that later in this chapter.

Churches are another resource for records, especially baptisms, weddings, and deaths. Having said that, please be considerate of the clergy and staff. They are faithfully and tirelessly tending to their flocks, and may not have the time or resources to assist you. Be polite and understanding of their response or lack thereof. Churches might be a better option when you actually go to your family's hometown.

Maybe you don't have the time or energy to conduct the research. Or, you've run into major roadblocks and don't know where to turn. There are organizations that will do the work for you. For example, My Italian Family[21] is one such service. Southern Italy Travel (mentioned in the next chapter) is an expert in small-town genealogical research. Organizations such as these can help you find records in other countries, and connect the dots, well, branches of your family tree.

CREATE

One way to create a *dolce vita* through genealogy is to visit a "Little Italy" near you. As you may know, most of our immigrant ancestors had to be "sponsored" to come to North America. Extended families often lived in the same tenement house, if not the same apartment.

Since family is one of the highest priorities in the Italian culture, it's no surprise that hardly anyone ever moved too far from home. For instance, Uncle Johnny moved from the first floor all the way to the second floor after he was married!

Even if our first-generation ancestors did move away from their parents' block, they still socialized in the Little Italy communities. They might've gone to the same coffee shop every day or joined an Italian club where they could play bocce and bask in the nostalgia of the Old Country.

On your genealogical quest, you're hoping to find people who personally knew your ancestors. But, there's no need to stress if you don't. You see, at the very least, you're learning about the culture which is the springboard to enriching your life today and for future generations.

Strike up a conversation at the bakery, or ask the butcher how to prepare that roast using a traditional method. Inquire about Italian social clubs or local newspapers. These are all valuable resources.

Here are some of the most popular Little Italy neighborhoods across North America:

- New York City—there are two: lower Manhattan and Arthur Avenue (the Bronx)
- Chicago, Illinois—Taylor Street (near West Side)
- Boston, Massachusetts—North End (part of the historic Freedom Trail)
- Providence, Rhode Island—Atwells Avenue (Federal Hill)
- Baltimore, Maryland—downtown, between the Inner Harbor and Fells Point
- Philadelphia, Pennsylvania—South Street
- San Diego, California—India Street (the largest "Little Italy" in the United States)
- Toronto, Canada—College Street West
- Montreal, Canada—Rosemont-La Petite-Patrie

For extensive information about and an ever-growing list of Italian American communities, from coast to coast, you'll love the Italian Enclaves Historical Society[22].

Genealogical research is taken to an entirely different level when you physically go where your ancestors were born. You'll be surprised at the emotions that arise when you're standing in Grandma's church or seeing Great-grandpa's initials on the wrought iron railing he made.

Even if you don't know if any relatives still live there, make the effort to visit your ancestor's town. Any stories you heard will come to life, and you'll feel a connection to a home you didn't know you were missing.

Be sure to bring photographs with you of your grandparents, aunts and uncles. Even with a language barrier, people will recognize faces. In fact, remember our cousin Sal mentioned earlier in this chapter? He and his wife did exactly that! They just showed up in our ancestors' town and started asking the locals if they recognized the people in the photos they brought. After a little while, they talked to enough people that they eventually found some cousins.

Another thing you could do before traveling to Italy is to check their White Pages (*Pagine Bianche*)[23]. If you have enough time before you leave for your trip, you could write or call those potential family members. If you feel a little awkward doing that, wait until you arrive and politely ask your hotel host to call them for you. For one thing, they speak the language better, and they might even know them.

Ancestry Alert! Before you reach out and touch someone, be prepared for the possible responses. Most of my husband's and my relatives welcomed us with open arms. There were, however, a few who were wary. Who can blame them? Some 'mericano shows up, out of the blue, claiming to be a long-lost relative. Sounds fishy, doesn't it?

The first time I went to Italy, with my father and Uncle Johnny, one of our cousins thought we were there to reclaim the land that my grandfather had given to them. With the help of a local relative, my father was able to assure this cousin that we were simply there to meet our family and connect to our roots. My dad was quite the diplomat!

Getting any documents, like birth certificates, could be easier when you're in the actual city of your ancestors. You can look up "comune" (town hall) to find out where it's located. There may also be instructions on how to request documents. Take note of office hours, especially if you're visiting during a weekend or near a holiday. Keep in mind that the records for some smaller towns might be kept in a larger town hall nearby.

When you arrive, you may need to show identification (like a passport), and they might ask why you want the documents. For example, if you're applying for dual citizenship, you'll need certified copies. More than likely, they'll need a day or so to prepare the documents.

When I visited the *Comune di Serrara Fontana*, I gave the clerk my grandfather's name and date of birth. He walked just a few steps away to a bookcase, pulled out a volume labeled "1895" and quickly found my grandfather's birth record. I thought it was funny that a century-old document was as handy as last week's town hall meeting notes.

As you view the records, be aware that some street names could have changed since your ancestors lived there. For example, the main street in my husband's grandfather's town changed after World War II; there's a plaque in the main square that explains the new name.

Some clues on documents may only be identified by a local. For example, on a birth certificate, the place of birth for my grandfather-in-law wasn't found on any map; it was a particular section of a street that only someone who was born and raised there would know. It's kind of like a Rhode Islander saying something is near the Civic Center or where Benny's used to be. If you're not from the Ocean State, you now know exactly what it's like to encounter mysterious locations on foreign documents.

CONTINUE

I can already hear some of you saying, "My grandkids aren't interested in family trees! They don't even like real trees. They're always looking at the Tic-Tac or the Instant-Grammar!"

Don't give up hope. They might not be interested today, but they very well could be in the future. When I was in my early teens, my father asked us kids if we'd ever want Grandpa's property in Italy. Stupidly, we said no and they gave it to a relative. What the h*ll were we thinking? We were short-sighted youngsters who were too busy with school, friends, and fun. Whenever I think about that, I try to remind myself (convince myself?) of the silver linings of not owning property in a foreign country...with a view of Capri and the Amalfi Coast...living a *dolce vita*...

Excuse me for a moment, I need to go cry in my pillow.

Okay. I'm back.

A simple way to plant seeds for your family's genealogical legacy is to point out similarities between the young generation and your ancestors. My friend Ann Marie does that. For example, she'll tell a niece how her great-grandmother had the same spirit of perseverance or musical talent. She'll remark how a nephew has the same facial expressions or sense of humor as their uncle. This makes our forebears more relevant and relatable, and may create curiosity about your family's history.

In addition to making a video about your family (Chapter 4), you could write a book. I heard you laugh, but seriously, it's not as overwhelming as you think. If your keyboard skills are hunt-and-peck, there's software that allows you to dictate your details. You or a family member can later edit it. You can then find someone (maybe on Fiverr) to design a cover and format the manuscript to upload to Amazon. Before you know it, your family's history will be available for all to read. Wow!

Retired gastroenterologist and Rhode Island Heritage Hall of Fame inductee, Dr. Ed Iannuccilli[24] did just that. He told the Providence Public Library, "The spark came one day while recounting my family's celebration of the Christmas Eve vigil to my oldest son. I realized how dear this and other memories were and how important they are for passing down knowledge, values, and meaningful traditions from one generation to the next." Dr. Iannuccilli went on to write several books—mostly memoirs—and often speaks on the subject of keeping your family history alive.

Genealogy is a key that unlocks the door to your past, revealing the roots that have shaped your present and will influence your future. It is a journey of discovery, a quest to understand who you are and where you come from. It's about understanding the cultures, traditions, and values that have been passed down through generations.

It also helps us to recognize the sacrifices our ancestors made for us to be where we are today. It's about appreciating the strength and resilience embedded in our DNA. It can provide a sense of belonging—a connection to something bigger than ourselves.

Genealogy is a bridge to your past and a compass for your future. So, embrace and learn from your family's history, and use that Key to Redeem Your Roots.

Key # 5: Genealogy Over the Top!

Italian Roots and Genealogy: Bob Sorrentino

In 2008, retired bank executive Bob Sorrentino began researching his Italian ancestry. Using some of the tools mentioned in this chapter, he was able to trace his Neapolitan roots back a thousand years!

Bob is the tireless creator of a blog, podcast, Facebook group, and YouTube channel dedicated to Italian genealogy.[25]

He has a wealth of resources for your genealogical journey, from research links and tools to books and a marketplace. There's even a section in his blog with authentic recipes.

Chapter 6

From Palazzos to Piazzas: Your Heritage through Travel

"The journey changes you; it should change you.
It leaves marks on your memory, on your
consciousness, on your heart.
You take something with you. Hopefully, you
leave something good behind."
~ Anthony Bourdain

Travel is a transformative experience that not only broadens your horizons but also deepens your understanding of your heritage. We can physically connect with our history, walk on the path our ancestors once tread, and breathe in the air of our forefathers' lands. Imagine standing in the very place where your great-grandparents were born, or gazing at Florence's Duomo as Michelangelo once did.

There's a profound sense of connection that comes from such experiences, a feeling of being part of a larger narrative that spans generations.

Our first trip to the ancestral home of my husband was a leap of faith since we didn't know anyone in the small town near Orvieto. Of the three possible contacts we had, none knew of any family in America. We happened to be there during the last week of May which is when the town celebrates the Feast of the Madonna. We gratefully accepted the invitation to participate.

The event started at the main church, and a procession, singing and praying, made its way to a tiny, charming chapel on a hill. After the outdoor mass, the scene was reminiscent of the loaves-and-fishes story of the New Testament: seemingly out of nowhere, long tables were suddenly piled high with all sorts of delectable dishes, and the homemade *prosecco* flowed like a fountain.

This is where we truly got to know the kind and loving people of San Michele in Teverina. Taking the time to talk, laugh, and eat together wove our hearts into the community. Since then, we've returned many times, and we stay in touch throughout the year. In fact, one of my husband's far-distant cousins now calls us *sanmichelesi* which means we're practically residents of that little town with great traditions, generosity, and love.

You, too, can have life-changing experiences when you travel to explore your heritage.

Little chapel in San Michele in Teverina (Lazio)

Post-service impromptu party

CONNECT

The first obstacles most people cite when it comes to travel are time and money. So, let's first take some baby steps: you can "go" to Italy without even leaving your couch! Then, we'll discuss other options that do require a passport.

The easiest way to connect to your heritage through travel is to do it virtually. There is an overwhelming number of travel videos online, in your local library, and on public television. (Who doesn't love Rick Steves?) You can also use Google Maps to "drive" through your great-grandparents' towns. If you have an address, plug that into the search box. How exciting to see the same view that they admired! At the very least, you can look up a landmark and go left and right, up and down from there.

Another giant virtual step is to hire someone to take you on a live video conferencing tour. There are many guides available for popular cities and sites such as Rome, Florence, and the Vatican. You simply arrange a day and time with the guide and they'll send you the connection information. Since the tour is live, you'll be able to ask questions. Check out Tours By Locals[26].

For those of us with families who came from dot-on-the-map towns in Italy, some companies will "take" you there via video. Southern Italy Travel specializes in genealogy-focused tours to the towns of your ancestors.[27] For those who are unable to fly there, they offer virtual tours, both live and pre-recorded. Additionally, Mirella at Southern Italy Travel can trace your family tree, and they can acquire the Italian vital records needed if you're applying for dual citizenship.

If you're ready to get a stamp in your passport, connecting means doing a little research about when and specifically where to go. Only you can make those choices. Do you love art? Then, Florence is for you. If you're a history buff, you don't want to miss Rome.

What if you want to visit your ancestors' small village in Italy? If you don't have any contacts there now, I'd suggest getting in touch with Mirella at Southern Italy Travel mentioned above. She can help organize a tour and you might even meet the mayor.

To tour or not to tour, that is the question!

One of the most common questions I get about visiting Italy is whether or not to take an organized tour or to go on your own. The answer is—drum roll, please!—maybe.

In my opinion, if you've never traveled outside of your country and your foreign language skills are lacking, I'd suggest taking an organized tour for your first trip to Italy. They'll take care of your hotels and intercity transportation, and show you the highlights of the most popular destinations. Tour guides also help overcome the language barrier.

The first time I went to Italy, we took an organized tour of Venice, Rome, and Florence. How cliché, right? But that whirlwind experience gave me an overview of each city and helped me decide where to live when I enrolled in an Italian language school a few years later.

Once you've done a tour or two, consider venturing out on your own. You'll go where you want when you want, and for however long you want. You'll also get to see off-the-beaten-path locations so you can experience a more authentic version of the country. Yes, it takes time and effort to research and then make reservations, but it will be worth it. I look at travel planning like a puzzle, fitting together all the pieces to create something beautiful.

CREATE

Be prepared: after your first trip, you might come down with a permanent case of wanderlust and be forever changed!

To create a life you love, I encourage you to be a traveler rather than a tourist.

Yes, there's a difference. A tourist just wants to check off the list of must-see places, putting another stamp in their passports. A traveler, on the other hand, wants to be immersed in the culture, learn about the people, and collect a lifetime of memories. There's nothing wrong with being a tourist. I realize sometimes time is a factor, and a half day is better than nothing. But, when possible, dive deeper.

> Italy first captures your attention. Then, it captures your heart.

To do this, make the effort to become what travel expert Rick Steves calls a "temporary local". For example, get tickets to a soccer game or at least watch one on the TV in a neighborhood bar. Follow your bar mates' cues about which team to root for! Take part in an evening stroll (*passeggiata*), or strike up a conversation with locals at a café. Be sure to stop by open-air markets for seasonal produce, home-baked treats, and maybe even some trendy fashions.

If you've never been to Italy before, it's wonderful to visit famous sites like the Colosseum, the Leaning Tower of Pisa, and Florence's Duomo. I'd always dreamed of seeing the ceiling of the Sistine Chapel with my own eyes. That dream came true and was even more special because my father and Uncle Johnny were by my side.

If you have a particular passion, like opera or fast cars, it's worth any effort to visit its mecca. Can you imagine watching *La Traviata* at La Scala in Milan? How about a tour of the Ducati factory near Bologna or driving a Ferrari on their test track? As a chocolate lover, one of my favorite experiences was taking a candy-making class at the world-famous Perugina *Casa del Cioccolato* (House of Chocolate) just outside of Perugia, Italy.[28]

You've probably figured out that we prefer traveling on our own and you might feel the same way. However, one tour you might consider involves two wheels: bicycle or motorcycle trips. You can find several companies that offer both guided and self-guided routes that take place in the region of your choice. In addition to the excitement of riding through Tuscan or Sicilian countryside, you get a more immersive experience of the areas. Many of the tour companies will transport your luggage between your overnight hotels. A dear friend of mine, Riccardo, met the love of his life on such a trip. So, you never know what could happen!

Something else to consider before making hotel reservations is the schedule of special events in the places on your itinerary. You might want to change the order of your trip or the length of time in a certain spot to coincide with a *gelato* festival or flag-throwing competition.

One travel topic that's even more divisive than the sauce-versus-gravy debate is whether to take a gondola ride in Venice or not. Yes, it's overpriced and the pinnacle of being touristy., will you regret it later if you don't? This is true for any of the stereotypical "must-see" stops on your vacation. If you love stained glass, for heaven's sake, go inside that church! If it doesn't float your boat (or gondola), don't bother.

Having said all that, I encourage you to get off the beaten path in those popular cities and venture out to the lesser-known areas of the Boot. That is where you'll experience the authentic Italy and, often not pay as much.

Two of my favorite online resources for Italian adventures are ItalyXP[29] and Viator.[30] (No, I don't get a commission. Darn it.) Both are reputable companies that contract with local vendors. I especially love ItalyXP's "Something Different" selections.

How do I find unique things to do and see? I do an internet search using these actual words: "unusual things to do in (place)." That's how we've driven vintage FIAT 500s along the Ligurian coast, motored through Tuscany on Vespas, and even taken gladiator lessons in Rome.

Are you starting to see how travel can create an amazing and memorable life?

CONTINUE

It doesn't take a genius to figure out the easiest way to continue your legacy through travel: invite your kids and grandkids to join you. Yes, it's easier said than done with everyone's schedules and—let's be frank—wallets.

For the most part, younger people love to travel and they prefer more authentic and even active experiences. So, how about taking a pasta-making class together? Also, that bicycle tour previously mentioned could be right up their alley.

You can easily find walking and hiking routes in almost every area. The town where my husband's family lives offers horseback riding and treks through the badlands. My family's island has stand-up paddleboards and a ropes course.

With almost 5,000 miles of coastline, Italy is a fantastic place to enjoy the water. Aside from beautiful beaches (especially Sardinia), expand your thinking and go whitewater rafting under the Tuscan sun, sailing in Liguria, or kitesurfing in Puglia.[31]

You might not be physically able to join them, but you'll be over the moon when they tell you all about their grand adventure at dinner.

The first time I visited Italy, I went with my father and uncle. So, in that case, I was the younger generation. I can speak from experience about how amazing and even life-changing traveling with your elders can be. In fact, my favorite memory of all time happened during those two weeks. I have a blurry photograph of my dad and Uncle Johnny leaning on a railing, soaking up the view that their parents had adored decades before. They were just hanging out together as brothers. Knowing that I played a small part in that happening makes me smile even today.

Another way to get the younger generation involved is through Study Abroad programs. Many US colleges and universities have "sister" institutions in Europe. Students can stay for a month or a semester. There are also cultural organizations that offer their own programs for their members. For example, the National Italian American Foundation (of which I'm a proud member) has an incredible two-week summer program[32] where students get all transportation, accommodations, meals, and tours.

Travel can open our eyes to new possibilities and perspectives, encouraging us to step out of our comfort zones and embrace new challenges. It can also provide us with a sense of purpose, as we keep the memory of our forefathers alive and pass on their stories to future generations.

Travel also allows us to immerse ourselves in the culture and traditions of not just our families, but the whole world as a global community. We can participate in seasonal festivals, taste traditional foods, and learn more about people in different countries. These experiences not only enrich our understanding of our heritage but also help us appreciate the diversity and richness of other cultures.

Isn't that the ultimate and ideal goal? We don't have to agree with someone else's views, but we can strive to respect one another. That's easier to do when we're open to understanding another perspective.

> "Perhaps travel cannot prevent bigotry, but by demonstrating that all peoples cry, laugh, eat, worry, and die, it can introduce the idea that if we try and understand each other, we may even become friends."
> ~ Maya Angelou

Key # 6: Travel Over the Top!

Our Italian Journey: Gary and Ilene Modica

Imagine falling in love with a place so much that you sell everything and move there. Award-winning authors and bloggers, Gary and Ilene Modica[33] of *Our Italian Journey*, did just that.

After the long rollercoaster ride to achieve dual citizenship, they lived in various parts of Italy over the course of a year to decide which town would become "home". Their travel-guide-meets-memoir first book will take you along for the exciting ride.

After a short return to the States, they moved to their new home in Lucca, Italy, where their adventures continue today and prompted their second book. Rumor has it that their third book is in the works and will highlight thirty towns in Tuscany. So, stay tuned!

Chapter 7

Andiamo! (Let's Go!): Your Heritage Through Associations

"We do not remember days;
we remember moments."
~ Cesare Pavese

To emulate the start of every Sicilian story of Sophia's from *The Golden Girls*, picture it: New York, 1905!

Although not in Sophia's land of Sicily, the Big Apple is where Vincenzo Sallaro and five other Italian immigrants held the first meeting of what is now known as the Order of the Sons and Daughters of Italy in America. They set up free schools in which to learn English and centers to help immigrants pursue citizenship. As the organization grew, it established orphanages and homes for the elderly as well as credit unions and scholarships.

Today, the OSDIA has thousands of members in all fifty states. As proud and patriotic Americans of Italian descent, they have donated millions to disaster relief, cultural preservation, scholarships, and fighting prejudices. Vincenzo and his friends probably never imagined that their little meeting in Little Italy would ever grow into such an influential organization. But, that's the power of people coming together with passion and purpose.

Now, the baton is passed to us as we look at the last Key to Redeem Your Roots. We'll take all we've discussed in this book, put it into action, and keep the momentum going. It's easier and more enjoyable to do that when you join forces with like-minded people. That's why this chapter's title is "*Andiamo!*" which means "Let's go!" It's not "I'm going" or "they're going." No, we are going to do this, so let's do it together.

Before we dive into how let's look at why it's important. And, it's not just for the sake of our heritage and traditions.

We humans are wired to be social, even those of us who are introverts. Think about some of the happiest and most meaningful moments in your life. I'll bet that you weren't alone for most of them.

Beyond the warmth and connection that we feel when we're with loved ones, research shows there are health benefits. An article from Harvard Medical School highlights some of these studies' findings:[34]

- Reduced risk of dementia

- Less cognitive decline

- Lower stress levels

- Boosted mood and feelings of value

- Longevity

While these studies aren't 100 percent conclusive in proving that socializing has health benefits, we can agree that it makes sense. We can also "do the math" and deduce that the opposite is also true: isolation can be detrimental to our health and happiness.

If you're not convinced, why not at least give it a try? It can't hurt and it could very well help.

CONNECT

Thankfully, there are so many organizations that teach and promote heritage, both virtually and in person. You can even find very specific groups such as those dedicated to food, language, or travel. Don't forget about demographics, such as associations for young adults or entrepreneurs. There's even an Italian American Baseball Foundation.[35]

Using the ethnicity of your choice, add an online search term such as *group* or *organization*. From there, you can go big or go home! What I mean is that you can then expand the search by adding words like *national* or *international*. Or shorten travel time by narrowing the search parameters to your city or state.

Here's a list—certainly not exhaustive—of some Italian associations. (Links are in the endnotes section of this book.[36])

- Order of the Sons and Daughters of Italy in America (OSDIA)

- National Organization of Italian American Women (NOIAW)

- National Italian American Foundation (NIAF)

- Italian American Future Leaders

- The Italian Language Foundation

- UNICO

- mi.o (modern italian online)

Another way to celebrate your heritage with others is to find out when feasts (annual holy days celebrating saints) and festivals are being held. They mostly happen in the summer and autumn and are often sponsored by a church. For example, the Saint Mary's Feast in Cranston, Rhode Island, has taken place each July for over 110 years. In New York City, the Feast of San Gennaro is celebrated every September.

These neighborhood parties offer food, fun, and fellowship for all ages. Though feast days are about more than just the dining delicacies, you can expect traditional dishes and desserts. Don't be surprised to see nuns making doughboys at the St Rocco's Feast in Johnston, Rhode Island! Fun comes in all varieties, from carnival games and raffles to music and dancing. But the best part is chatting with your new *paesani* (friends) which makes you feel more connected to the community.

As a note, the term "feast" comes from the Italian word *festa* which means party. For my Greek friends, you could look for a *glendi*, and

Portuguese partiers might attend a LaLa. Those of you with Scottish origins, don your kilt and head out for the Highland Games.

Don't forget one of the pioneers of bringing like-minded people together on an international scale: Meetup.com.[37] Everywhere I've lived, I've always signed up with a local chapter. For example, there are more than 100 Italian culture and language groups worldwide as of this writing.

Hmmm...there's not one near you? You could start one like we did in Kansas City. Yes, it takes some time and energy, but it's so rewarding. My friend Sheila and I had our first meeting with a handful of others and over time membership grew to hundreds. We hosted film series, wine tastings, cooking classes, and multiple conversation groups throughout the metropolitan area.

If we did it, you can, too!

CREATE

Now that you've discovered all these organizations and feasts, it's time to take action. Become a member of the groups that interest you the most and attend their next event. Mark your calendar for that local feast this summer. Buy tickets to the Italian Heritage Night at your Major League Baseball stadium.

What if there aren't any of these cultural opportunities near you? Then you get to embody the "create" part of this chapter and make them come to life. How? By being a pioneer and making it happen.

It could be as simple as inviting friends over for pizza or, if you're feeling ambitious, making pasta together. Get a bocce set and learn to play in your yard or at a local park. How about an Italian-themed book club? They could be fiction, memoirs, or travel-based. There are a myriad of books about the Little Italy neighborhoods across the country and many about the immigrant experience. You might even ask the author if they'd consider popping in for a video chat when you meet. Hey, the worst they can say is no, right?

How about watching a movie together like *Cinema Paradiso* and discussing it later—over snacks, of course. You could even step that up a notch by booking a room at a local library in which to show the film and inviting the cardholders. If food and drink are allowed, encourage attendees to bring something to share.

My friends Rachel and Stephen, who I met in Colorado, had a genius idea for getting people together around an ethnic theme. We had a group of six to eight people and one person or couple would host that month's dinner. The host picked the theme (Greek, Hawaiian, etc.) and made the main dish. Everyone else brought side dishes and desserts. Not only did it spread out the hosting duties and all the prep work that goes into that, but we also got to try new foods and learn about other cultures. Doesn't it figure that the month they chose an Italian theme, I was in Italy? Oh, well.

You can take Rachel and Stephen's idea and make it a little easier. Perhaps you and your friends simply host a pizza party, and everyone brings one with different toppings. (Remember, for the love of all things holy, do not bring pineapple!) Or how about a dessert and coffee get-together? You could even host your own Build-a-Charcuterie Bash: everyone brings a selection of meat or cheese and some fruit, and you all assemble it together.

By the way, Italians have been serving charcuterie boards forever. What? Yes, *charcuterie* is just a fancy French way of saying *antipasto*. It's all good. We don't mind that the French are getting all the credit these days. We know who started it.

Contrary to popular belief, getting together doesn't have to revolve around food. You could all attend a concert, see a movie, or go dancing together. My friend Riccardo has a bocce court in his backyard where friends gather during the summer.

When is a good time to create our *dolce vita* with other people? Now! Or maybe even yesterday! If we keep saying we'll do it "someday", it'll never happen. Then, a week becomes a month that becomes a year, and then we wonder why we feel disconnected. Worse, if everyone waits for "next month," that restaurant or cultural group might not be around due to a lack of interest. Don't let that happen!

CONTINUE

Which would you prefer?

A) having someone drone on and on about why you must be interested in what they love

or

B) being invited to a party with like-minded people, great food, and fun?

Even if you're an introvert, you probably chose B. That's because no one wants to have something shoved in their face even if it's amazing. Furthermore, who wouldn't want to hang out with people who share our interests and have a good time? Throwing in some cannoli doesn't hurt, either.

It's the same with the next generation. If we want them to continue our family's legacy, it needs to be appealing to them. I'm certainly not saying you have to dress like Gen-whatever-letter-we're-on-now or listen to their music. (Ouch, my ears!). It's important to make it appealing to them.

Do you remember *Schoolhouse Rock*? It taught us everything from grammar to how laws are made. Is "Conjunction Junction" or "I'm Just a Bill" now stuck in your head? If so, you understand the power of learning something in a fun way, and you realize how deeply it makes an impact. No *sittin' here on Capitol Hill* required.

Including the next generation in these group activities is the Trojan horse that brings our heritage into their lives. It's not being sneaky; it's being effective. It's not like you're trying to slip in something evil or harmful. Instead, you're simply finding the best way to spark interest in something you know will benefit them.

Then, it will be their turn to CONNECT to their heritage, CREATE their *dolce vita*, and CONTINUE their legacy for the future. You'll be glad that they will and that they, too, will do it together.

Key #7: *Andiamo!*
Over the Top

Sons and Daughters of Italy Colombo in Omaha, Nebraska

Imagine having *Nonna* (Grandma) make her famous meatballs and pasta for you. Can you smell the simmering sauce? Can you picture her bustling around making sure everyone has enough to eat?

That's pretty much what happens at the Sons and Daughters of Italy Lodge in Omaha, Nebraska.[38] The difference is that it's not just one grandma, but a host of volunteers who make the magic happen. They start early in the week cutting and seasoning the meat to make fresh sausage. Then, the organized chaos begins as dinner is served on Thursdays and Fridays.

The Sons and Daughters of Italy originally started to help Italians integrate into the American culture. Having met that goal, their mission now is to keep the Italian culture and heritage alive. They also give back to the community by donating to charities and sponsoring scholarships.

The key? They do it together. The guests and volunteers alike benefit from the sense of nostalgia and community. It's not just a meal, but, an echo from the past. As one attendee said, "I feel like my grandma just made me dinner!"

Chapter 8

Avanti! (Go Forth!)

Uncle Mike, my grandmother's youngest brother, was a kind soul with a twinkle in his eye. I'm grateful for all the times I was able to visit him on the Italian island of Ischia. We'd walk around the family's huge property as he pointed out the fruit trees, gardens, livestock, and—of course—the wine cellars carved into the rock. The doors and padlocks looked like props from a Medieval movie set.

One of my fondest memories of Uncle Mike was during the *vendemmia* (grape harvest). Even though he was at an advanced age, he was there with his sons pressing the grapes and loving every minute. Doing it the old-school, manual way was hard work, but he never lost his smile.

He was the only one of my grandmother's siblings who immigrated to America and returned after six months. He missed his family and his home. When my father learned that, he looked out from Uncle Mike's terrace with a view of the sparkling sea and said to him, "You chose well."

Every time we'd have to part ways, Uncle Mike took my hands, kissed both of my cheeks, and said, "*Tante belle cose.*" The literal translation is "many beautiful things," but it means so much more. Uncle Mike was telling me that he wished the best for me and the family in the States, that happiness and good health poured down on us, and that God would bless us. Three little words—*tante belle cose*—packed with a lifetime of love.

Why did I just tell you about my Uncle Mike? You could guess a few reasons related to this book and they'd probably all be correct. Yet, the real reason I share a few glimpses of him is to prove a point.

Five minutes ago, you had no idea who Michele "Mike" Iacono of Calimera, Ischia, was. But now you do. That's the power of talking about those who came before us. It brings them to life today and keeps their memory relevant for the next generation. You don't have to be a master storyteller. You just have to tell their story.

Never forget that our parents and grandparents are worthy of being remembered. We're grateful for the hard work and sacrifices they made for us, and we can learn from the hardships and failures that they faced. Heroes don't always wear capes; they wear aprons, fedoras, slippers, and even motorcycle jackets.

There's one more point that I'd like to make about our heritage and it has to do with choices.

Have you ever heard how we become who we associate with? Whether it's income, beliefs, or fashion, we tend to become like the people in our day-to-day circle. As we're continually exposed to, let's say, skirt hemlines or sociological beliefs, we adopt them as our own. Or, at the very least, we accept them. Yes, this could be good or bad.

So, what does that have to do with our ethnicity? Glad you asked!

John Maxwell, New York Times best-selling author and leadership mentor, said, "We are all tattooed in the crib with the beliefs of our tribe. When we are growing up, we soak up not only all the good, but also all the bad of what is going on around us."

He goes on to say that we aren't responsible for any baggage from our childhood. However, we are responsible for changing that baggage if we want something different in the future.

For example, I sometimes hear my fellow Italian Americans say, "I can't help it. I'm Italian!" Along with hands flying up in the air, those words are often exclaimed after doing something inappropriate.

No, *amico mio* (my friend), you *can* help it.

The scientific jury is still out when it comes to the question of personality traits being embedded in our DNA. So, blaming bad behavior on genetics is a cop-out.

We may have grown up with ideas that clash with how we want our lives to be. Just like an arborist prunes branches for the sake of the tree, you and I can decide what parts of our heritage will benefit us today. We get to choose the direction for ourselves and for generations to come.

Picture one of those old steamer trunks that our grandparents packed for their journey to America. Over the years, they were filled with linens, photographs, and various mementos.

When grandparents pass away, some heirs keep the trunk and keep it closed. Others open it like a treasure chest and then go on to use Grandma's tablecloth and display Grandpa's military medals.

The saddest choice would be to just haul it out to the curb on trash day.

Our heritage and traditions are like that steamer trunk. Maybe you never explored your roots. That's okay because you can start now. Perhaps you're embracing some of your family's practices but others just don't fit. That's also okay. Even if you pull some things out and leave others inside, you're keeping the steamer trunk relevant and unlocked.

Please, don't carelessly discard your family history. Your ancestors made sacrifices so you could be where you are today. At the very least, they deserve your attention and respect.

What you do with the contents of your figurative steamer trunk is up to you. At least you honored your family by considering their legacy. Now, it's time to build yours.

Through the 7 Keys of this book, we've explored profound ways to CONNECT with our heritage, CREATE a life of meaning and purpose, and CONTINUE the legacy our ancestors began. This journey has been about more than just uncovering the past; it's about weaving those threads into the fabric of our present and future.

By connecting to our roots, we gain a deeper understanding of who we are and where we come from. This connection provides a foundation of strength, wisdom, and resilience that can guide us through life's challenges. It's a reminder that we are part of something much bigger than ourselves—a vibrant tapestry of history, culture, and tradition.

Creating a life you love involves exploring this connection to make choices that resonate with you. It's about embracing your passions, holding true to your values, and cultivating relationships that uplift and inspire you. By integrating your heritage into the day-to-day, you create a sense of continuity and purpose that enriches your life and those around you.

Continuing the legacy is an act of love, respect, and responsibility. It's about preserving the treasures of the past while also being open to new experiences and growth. This balance ensures that the legacy you pass on is dynamic and relevant, a living testament to the enduring power of heritage.

As you move forward (*avanti*), remember that this journey is ongoing. Continue to explore, learn, and grow. Let your roots nourish you, your creativity ignite you, and your legacy inspire future generations.

Your heritage is a powerful gift—cherish it, celebrate it, and let it guide you toward a life of fulfillment and purpose.

Appendix: Action Steps to Redeem Your Roots

For those of you who want a step-by-step, abbreviated plan to Redeem Your Roots, this is for you. Some of the suggested steps are questions to be answered.

This list can be used to start and then guide a group, either with your family or others who share your passion.

As you know, this process won't happen by itself and there is no Heritage Fairy. (I wish!) To make sure you take action, put time in your calendar to follow these steps. If you see your heritage quest like an appointment, it won't get pushed off to "someday".

Introduction: The Importance of Redeeming Your Roots

1) Why do you want to connect to your heritage?

2) What are some traditions that stand out in your memory?

3) Why do you think it's important that the next generation learns about their roots?

4) If you didn't grow up with a strong sense of heritage, why are you exploring it now?

Chapter 1: Mangia! (Eat!) Your Heritage through Food

1) What are your favorite ethnic dishes? Plan to enjoy them at least once a week.

2) Go to some authentic restaurants or markets in your area. If they're difficult to find, there are many online resources to bring those specialties to your doorstep.

3) Find at least one new recipe to make. When possible, include the younger generation.

Chapter 2: Eat, Pray, Love, and Eat Some More: Your Heritage through Holidays and Traditions

1) What is the next major holiday? Choose one or two traditions that you'll include. It could be something you want to revive or one to try for the first time.

2) Find out when your loved one's onomastico (name day) is, and plan how you'll celebrate.

3) For the next holiday, figure out how will you invite your children, grandchildren, nieces, and nephews to get involved.

Chapter 3: You Had Me at "Ciao!" Your Heritage through Language

1) Start to use simple phrases in your everyday life. For example, say "Grazie!" ("Thank you!") to the person behind the counter or "Che bello!" ("How nice!") when someone shares good news.

2) Sign up for live language lessons or download an on-demand course.

3) Teach the younger generation some words and phrases. You know it's easier to learn when they're young!

Chapter 4: Serenades and Silver Screens: Your Heritage through Music and Film

1) Tune in to an online Italian or other international radio station. Don't be surprised if you hear a lot of American music!

2) Watch online videos of famous singers and groups from your family's country of origin. They could be from days gone by or contempo-

rary artists. Often, the videos include the lyrics. A quick online translation will unravel the musical mystery for you.

3) Download, stream, or borrow from your local library a film with actors such as Sophia Loren, Roberto Benigni, or Marcello Mastroianni. For cannoli points (versus brownie points), watch your favorite English-speaking movie but turn on the foreign language subtitles or dubbing.

4) To find musicians for the younger generation, check out the performers from this year's Sanremo Music Festival, Eurovision, or other international song competitions. Many new artists are discovered on those prestigious stages. You might just *happen* to play some of their tunes while your nieces and nephews are in the car with you, wink wink!

Chapter 5: Branching Out: Your Heritage through Genealogy

1) Start creating your family tree, going back as far as you can. You get cannoli points if you have photos.

2) Ask your relatives if they can fill in the blanks on the branches of your family tree. It's not just

about names and dates. Ask them to share their memories of your ancestors.

3) If you're lucky enough to have older family members still alive, please, please, please record them. Not only will it help you preserve their words, but also their spirit.

4) Ask the younger generation to help you with the technology side of genealogy.

Chapter 6: From Palazzos to Piazzas: Your Heritage through Travel

1) Watch videos about where your ancestors came from. Notice the scenery, the people interacting, the food, and the sounds.

2) Do some research: where would you stay, what time of year would you go, and what would you want to see? Are the famous landmarks important to you? Why or why not?

3) Ask your children, grandchildren, nieces, and nephews what they'd like to see and do in the Old Country.

Chapter 7: Andiamo! (Let's Go!): Your Heritage through Associations

1) Find out when the next local feast or festival takes place and put it on the calendar.

2) Join one or two organizations that align with your interests. Commit to getting involved.

3) Use Rachel and Stephen's technique of hosting an ethnic potluck dinner, or a coffee-and-dessert party.

4) Invite the younger generation to help plan and pull off that dinner or party.

Endnotes

1. "The Stories That Bind Us," The New York Times, March 2013 https://www.nytimes.com/2013/03/17/fashion/the-family-stories-that-bind-us-this-life.html; Diahan Southard, "Why Children Should Learn Family History": https://www.yourdnaguide.com/ydgblog/why-children-learn-family-history

2. Michael Graziano, "Tapping into Strengths," *Psychotherapy Networker Magazine*, May/June 2008, https://www.psychotherapynetworker.org/article/tapping-strengths/

3. Italian American Future Leaders: https://www.iafuture.org/

4. Blue Zones: https://www.bluezones.com/

5. Pasquale Sciarappa: https://www.facebook.com/OrsaraRecipes/

6. Cucinamore https://www.cucinamore.net/

7. Traveling Italian Chef: https://www.travelingitalianchef.com/index.php

8. Chef Ezio of Ciao Abruzzo Tours: https://ciaoabruzzo.com/

9. Nonna Live online Italian cooking classes: https://nonnalive.com/

10. Bella Napoli, Kansas City, Missouri: https://kcbellanapoli.com/

11. The Italian Mass Project New York: https://www.facebook.com/ItalianMassProjectNY/

12. LearnAmo: https://www.youtube.com/@LearnAmo

13. EfficaceMente (con Andrea Giuliodori): https://www.youtube.com/@EfficaceMente

14. Bedford Italian Cultural Society (BICS): https://newbics.org/

15. Scuola Leonardo da Vinci (Italian language schools with locations throughout northern Italy): https://www.scuolaleonardo.com/

16. Italian Film Festival USA: https://italianfilm-fests.org/

17. Florida Atlantic University Italian Studies: https://www.fau.edu/artsandletters/llcl/italian/

18. Live worldwide radio stations app: http://radio.garden

19. Margie Raimondo and Urbana Farmstead: https://www.urbanafarmstead.net

20. Ellis Island Foundation Passenger Search: https://heritage.statueofliberty.org/

21. My Italian Family: https://www.myitalianfamily.com/

22. Italian Enclaves Historical Society: www.ItaliaEnclaves.org

23. Pagine Bianche (Italian White Pages): https://www.paginebianche.it/

24. Dr Ed Iannuccilli, Providence Public Library: https://www.provlib.org/ppl-alum/dr-ed-iannuccilli/

25. Bob Sorrentino of Italian Roots and Genealogy: https://www.italiangenealogy.blog/

26. Tours By Locals: https://www.toursbylocals.com/

27. Southern Italy Travel: https://www.southernitalytravel.com/

28. Casa del Cioccolato museum and school in Perugia: https://www.perugina.com/it/casa-del-cioccolato/Welcome-to-the-Casa-del-Cioccolato

29. ItalyXP: https://italyxp.com/en

30. Whitewater rafting (and other adventures) in Tuscany: https://www.destinationflorence.com/en/12-outdoor/123-adventure

31. Whitewater rafting (and other adventures) in Tuscany: https://www.destinationflorence.com/en/12-outdoor/123-adventure

32. NIAF Voyage of Discovery (for students): https://www.niaf.org/programs/voyage-of-discovery/

33. Our Italian Journey: https://ouritalianjourney.com/

34. Heidi Godman, "Get Back Your Social Life to Boost Thinking, Memory, and Health," *Harvard Health Letter*, October 22, 2023, https://www.health.harvard.edu/mind-and-mood/get-back-your-social-life-to-boost-thinking-memory-and-health

35. Italian American Baseball Foundation: https://iabf.foundation/

36. Italian cultural and heritage organizations:

37. Meetup.com Italian groups: https://www.meetup.com/topics/italian/

38. Sons and Daughters of Italy in Omaha, Nebraska: https://sonsofitalyne.org/

Glossary of Italian Words and Phrases

amici (ah-MEE-chee): friends, either all men or a group of both men and women

andiamo (on-dee-AH-mo): we are going. With an exclamation point, it means "Let's go!"

arrangiarsi (ah-rahn-jee-ARR-see): literally, to arrange oneself. Figuratively, it means to make the most out of a challenging situation and often in a clever way. In other words, when life gives you lemons, make *limoncello*!

avanti (ah-VAHN-tee): forward, ahead. With an exclamation point, it means "Go forth!". It was also the title of a 1972 comedy with Jack Lemmon.

caffè sospeso (kah-FEH soh-SPEH-szoh): literally translated, it means "suspended coffee." But it's really a Neapolitan custom of purchasing two coffees and taking only one; the other is "suspended" (as in waiting) for someone down on their luck to enjoy later.

campanilismo   (kom-pah-nee-LEEZ-moh): from the Italian word for bell tower, it's a sense of pride and respect for one's hometown.

cane (KAH-neh): dog

che bello (KEH BELL-oh): how nice!

che bel profumo (KEH BELL pro-FOOM-oh): what a wonderful aroma!

ciao (CHOW): hi or bye, and only used informally. Comes from the Venetian phrase *s-ciào vostro*, literally meaning "(I am) your slave", similar to the English "at your service". Never use this when you want to be respectful.

comune (koh-MOO-neh): as a noun, town or town hall; as an adjective, it means common.

dolce vita (DOHL-cheh VEE-tah): literally translated "sweet life." And implies a life of happiness, a good life.

festa (FEH-stah): party. In North America, the word is anglicized to *feast* meaning big Italian carnivals that happen during the good weather months

frigo (FREE-goh): fridge. short for refrigerator—*frigorifero* (free-go-REE-feh-roh). Yeah, let's stick with *frigo*!

gelato (jeh-LAH-toh): Italy's richer, creamier cousin to ice cream. When in Italy, it's a law to have one gelato a day. Okay, I made that up, but I still uphold the law.

Gesù (jeh-ZOO): Jesus

grazie (GRATZ-ee-eh): thank you

la bella figura (lah BEH-lah fee-GOO-rah): literally translated as "the beautiful figure," it implies an important social grace in Italy: making a good impression.

la bella lingua (lah BEH-lah LEEN-gwah): literally translated as "the beautiful language," it implies the Italian language.

latte (LAH-the): milk. not to be confused with a *caffè latte* which is coffee with milk.

la vita è bella (lah VEE-tah eh BEH-lah): "life is beautiful." also the name of the 1997 award-winning film by Roberto Benigni.

limoncello (lee-mohn-CHEL-loh): a liqueur made from lemon zest always served chilled; often served after dinner as a digestive.

mangia/mangiamo (MAHN-jah/mahn-jee-AH-moh): "he or she is eating/we are eating," with an exclamation point, it's in the imperative mood and means (you) eat/let's eat!

'mericano (meh-ree-KAH-no): American. Neapolitans often truncate the first syllable of this word. Another version is *medigan* [meh-dee-GHAN] which is even further from the original but easier to say if you can't roll your r's.

moppine (mah-PEEN): Italian-American slang for dishcloth. Like *paesano*, most speakers drop the last syllable from *moppina*. Did you see that Rachael Ray sells Moppine kitchen towels?

mutande (moo-TAHN-deh): underwear.

nonna (NAW-nah): grandma

onomastico (oh-noh-MAS-tee-koh): name day, usually, a saint's day like March 17 is Saint Patrick's Day. There's no green beer in Italy, though anyone named Patrick or Patricia is celebrated and might even get presents on that day. By the way, there's proof that the patron saint of Ireland was Roman.

paesano (pie-eh-ZAH-noh): fellow country-man. Colloquially, the final vowel is truncated, so you'll often hear *paesan* [pie-ZAHN].

Pagine Bianche (PAH-gee-neh bee-AHN-keh): White Pages for addresses and phone numbers.

passeggiata (pah-seh-JAH-tah): a leisurely stroll, especially in the evening, a time to see and be seen in the neighborhood.

peposa (peh-POH-zah): Tuscan braised beef stew.

porchetta (por-KEH-tah): seasoned pork loin, and my husband's must-have foods while in Italy

tante belle cose (TAHN-teh BEH-leh COZ-eh): literally translated as "many beautiful things," it implies wishes for health, happiness, blessings, and love.

vendemmia (vehn-DAME-mee-uh): grape harvest

About the Author

Award-winning and Best-Selling Author, Keynote Speaker & Certified Life Coach

For over twenty-five years, Dawn Mattera Corsi has been helping people create a *dolce vita* by connecting to their purpose and by continuing their legacy.

A former engineer, Dawn is also a best-selling and award-winning and best-selling author, a certified coach, and a keynote speaker. Her communication style offers proven techniques, heartfelt empathy, and a dash of tough love!

Within the span of a few years, she was divorced, was laid off twice, moved three times, and faced the most challenging emotional and financial difficulties of her life. Rather than sink into old patterns of depression, Dawn overcame despair to design a life of passion, peace, and purpose.

She has spoken for the American Cancer Society, March of Dimes, WeightWatchers, and a defense industry contractor. A regular guest on CBS and Fox News, she has been featured in numerous media outlets.

Dawn and her husband, Bob, have taken gladiator lessons in Rome and driven vintage Vespas through Tuscany. Her research for the best gelato continues.

Connect with Dawn:
Website: www.YourDolceVita.com
Facebook: @DawnAlbaMattera
Instagram: @dawnmatteraauthor
LinkedIn: https://www.linkedin.com/in/dawn-mattera-corsi-1309bb6/

If you loved this book, then you'll love...

The Italian Art of Living
Your Passport to Hope, Happiness, and
Your Personal Renaissance

NOW IS THE TIME TO TRANSFORM YOUR LIFE
WITH PASSION AND PURPOSE

Do you feel like the world is plummeting into darkness and despair? Are you struggling to stay optimistic and tired of only existing?

If so, *The Italian Art of Living* is your passport to a happier, hopeful, and more meaningful life. With clarity and encouragement, author Dawn Mattera translates the Italian tenacity and passion for life into practical lessons. But hold on to your cannoli! This isn't about gondolas and pasta, but rather a guide to triumphing over trials, moving forward with hope, and encouraging others to join you.

The keys to *The Italian Art of Living* include:

- Rising above challenges, fears, and excuses so you can achieve your dreams

- Triumphing over depression and unforgiveness to break free from the past

- Discovering your priorities and purpose so you can make a difference

- Embracing the best of your heritage to create a meaningful legacy

DON'T WAIT ANOTHER DAY FOR A RENAISSANCE IN YOUR LIFE!

Available wherever books are sold.

Invite Dawn to Speak at Your Next Event!

With decades of experience in leadership, training, public relations, wellness, and education, Dawn will empower your organization to achieve goals and stay motivated.

A regular guest on CBS and Fox News, Dawn has spoken for the American Cancer Society, March of Dimes, WeightWatchers, numerous online summits, and a defense industry contractor.

Available for in-person and virtual events

Topics include:

LEAD
For Corporations and Non-Profit Groups
Based on The Success Principles®
From Burnout to Breakthrough: Wellness and High Performance
Resilience and Retention in Tough Times

LIVE
For people over 50—It's never too late!

5 Keys to a Dolce Vita in Your 50s and Beyond
Dawn can inspire you to create a *dolce vita* (sweet life) as she shares how to:

BELIEVE that you're never too old to find fulfillment
DISCOVER the skills to put your plan into action
MAKE a difference

LEGACY
For people who want to:

CONNECT to their heritage
CREATE a richer life
CONTINUE their legacy
Redeem Your Roots: Keys to Bridge the Gap from Nostalgia to the Next Generation

International Best-Selling Anthology Books

The Keys To Authenticity with Jack Canfield
Unlocking the Code to a Fulfilling Life and Business
Editor's Choice Award

Rise Up! with Lisa Nichols
Ignite Your Inner Fire with Stories of Courage and Commitment

The Transformation Within
Words of Wisdom from a Collection of Coaches to Help You Win at the Game of Life

Available on Amazon: